A TREASURY OF

CELTIC DESIGN

Other titles illustrated by Courtney Davis

The Celtic Art Source Book

The Celtic Tarot, Courtney Davis and Helena Paterson

Celtic Iron-on Transfer Book

Symbols of the Grail Quest, Forester Roberts and Courtney Davis

Merlin Awakes, Peter Quiller and Courtney Davis

Celtic Gods, Celtic Goddesses, R.J.Stewart, Miranda Gray and Courtney Davis

Celtic Designs and Motifs

The Encyclopaedia of Arthurian Legends, Ronan Coghlan and Courtney Davis

Celtic Borders and Decoration

The Irish Celtic Magical Tradition, Steve Blamires and Courtney Davis

The Celtic Stained Glass Colouring Book

The Art of Celtia

Celtic Myths, Celtic Legends, R.J.Stewart and Courtney Davis

Celtic Mandalas, Courtney Davis and Helena Paterson

King Arthur's Return, Courtney Davis and Helena Paterson

The Book of Celtic Saints, Courtney Davis and Elaine Gill

Celtic Image, Courtney Davis and David James

Celtic Ornament: The Art of the Scribe

Celtic Women, Lyn Webster Wilde and Courtney Davis

Celtic Pilgrimages, Elaine Gill, Davis Everett and Courtney Davis

Celtic Initials and Alphabets

Celtic Illumination : The Irish School

St Patrick: A Visual Celebration, Courtney Davis, Elaine Gill and Dennis O'Neill

A TREASURY OF CELTIC DESIGN

Courtney Davis

Constable · London

First published in Great Britian 1999 by Constable and Company Ltd
3 The Lanchesters, 162 Fulham Palace Road, London W6 9ER
Copyright © 1999 Courtney Davis
ISBN 0 09 478730 1
The right of Courtney Davis to be identified as the author of this work has been
asserted by him in accordance with the Copyright, Designs and Patents Act 1988
Printed in Great Britain by St Edmundsbury Press Ltd, Bury St Edmunds, Suffolk

A CIP catalogue record for this book is available from the British Library

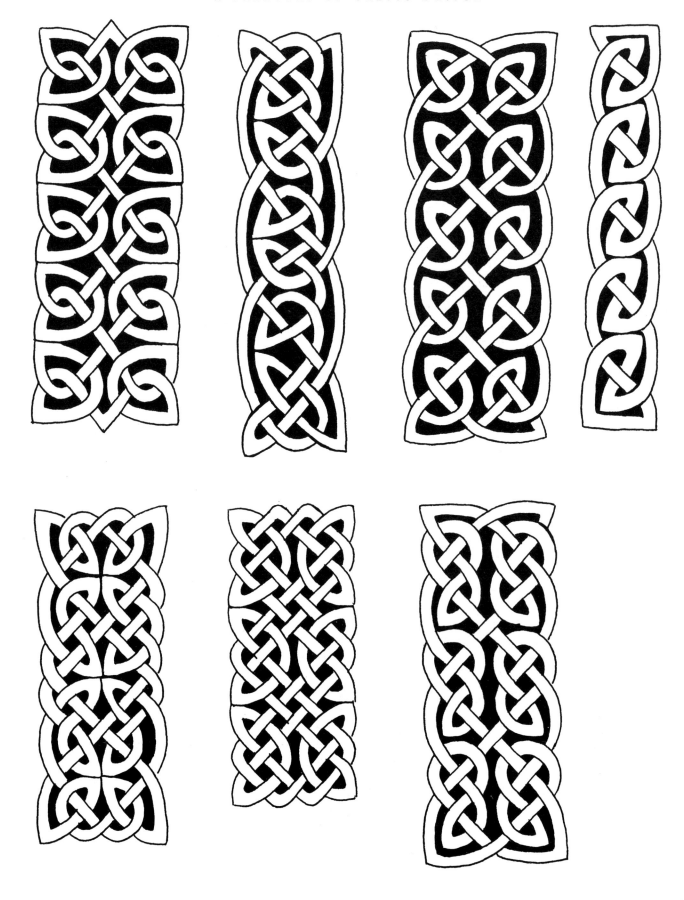

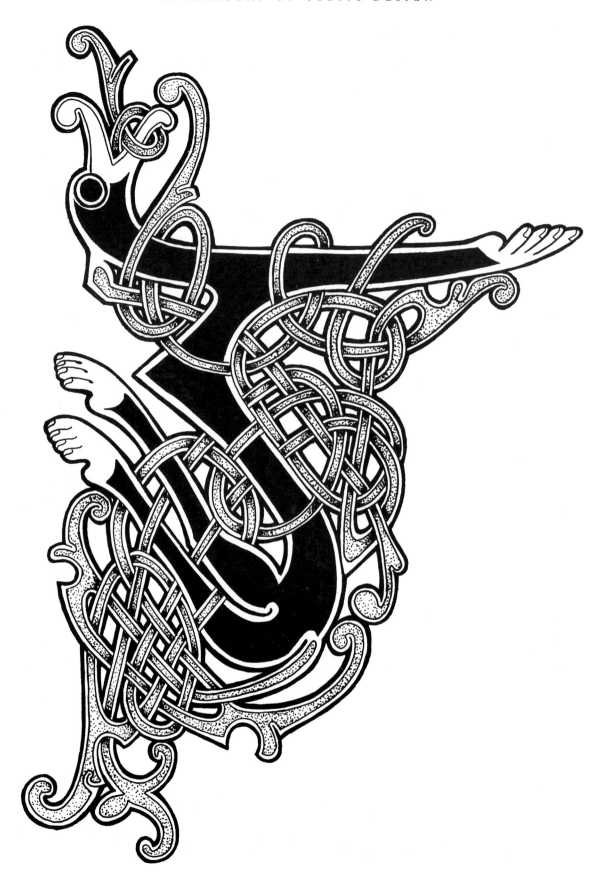

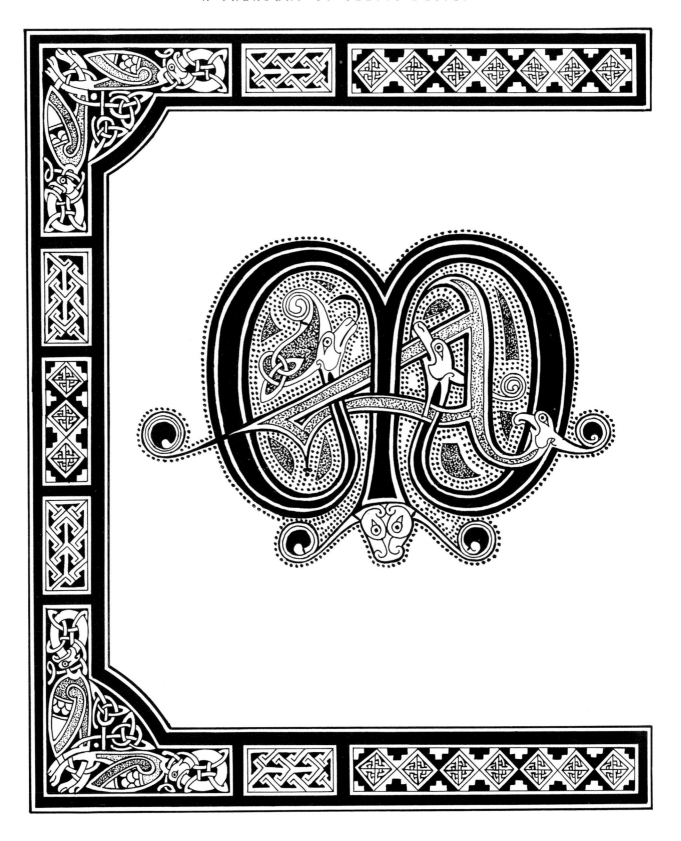